THE
GROWN-ASS
WOMEN'S
CLUB

Be Awesome.
Earn Badges.

ILLUSTRATIONS BY
LYDIA ORTIZ

CHRONICLE BOOKS
SAN FRANCISCO

introduction

Have you ever been proud of yourself and your accomplishments, only to be met with the snide reply, "What do you want, a cookie?"

This is an absurd question. Of course you want a cookie. Who doesn't want a cookie? And why shouldn't a Grown-Ass Woman be rewarded for the things she does?

This journal is dedicated to giving you the (metaphorical) cookies you deserve for everything you do, everything you put up with, and everything you achieve as you make your way through this extended school vacation we call adulthood.

Waited in a long line just to buy a salad because you know it's the healthier option? You deserve recognition! Smiled sweetly about your

work and money

$

BADGE of HONOR

MARKET WATCH 143.4

ABT 36.2 ACL 32.3 SH

AWARDED TO MYSELF FOR:

investing

DATE ISSUED: _____

ACCOMPLISHMENT: _____

_____

_____

_____

_____

_____

_____

$$$ THE
pay my automobills
BADGE

The freedom of adulthood means having your own apartment, your own car, and your own lights and heating and cable TV—but eventually the bills come due. Well, you can only assume they do, because you've figured out the true secret of bill paying: autopay.

Of course, it is advisable to stay aware and awake for all of the comings and goings from your bank account (because hey, if there's no money to withdraw, autopay is meaningless), but that doesn't mean you shouldn't pat yourself on the back for enrolling. With autopay you don't have to worry about that creepy neighbor who steals your mail (it's a federal offense, Mr. Hennings!) or running out of checks because you tried to get the backordered ones with the zodiac signs on them or being late with your payment. Give yourself an auto-high five for making sure that you've thought ahead and preemptively taken care of those bills.

Even if you skip the service but manage to nail those bills every month yourself, well, then you're the autopay. Whoa.

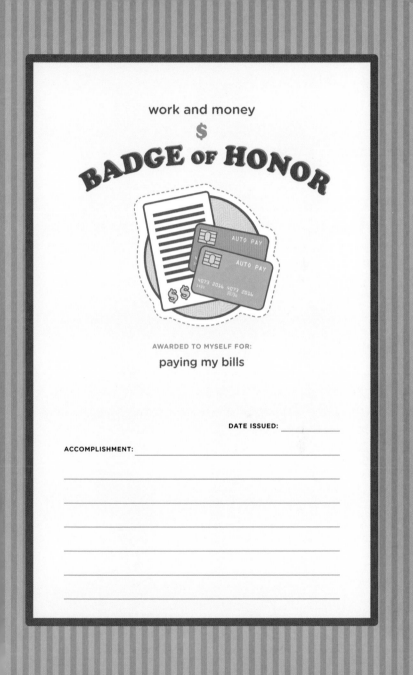

work and money

$

BADGE OF HONOR

AWARDED TO MYSELF FOR:

paying my bills

DATE ISSUED: _____

ACCOMPLISHMENT: _____

_____

_____

_____

_____

_____

_____

red alert

The average woman shows up to do her job with cramps, back pain, and a steady stream of blood expelling itself from her body *twelve times a year*. There should be workman's' comp for that time of the month. But, until we get there, this badge will have to honor us for dragging our tired, bloated, bitchy selves into the office, month after month, and doing that crap with a smile—or at least a really friendly sneer.

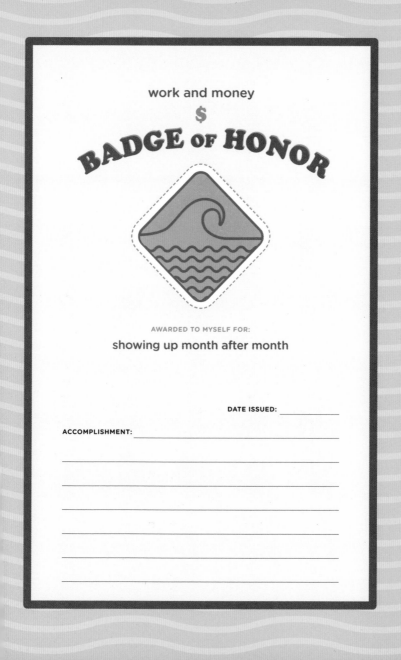

work and money

$

BADGE OF HONOR

AWARDED TO MYSELF FOR:

showing up month after month

DATE ISSUED: _____

ACCOMPLISHMENT: _____

_____

_____

_____

_____

_____

_____

THE
red flag
BADGE
of courage

Your new suitor seems great, mostly. He's smart and handsome or she's funny and good at picking restaurants. And you really want to be open to people and not jump to conclusions. But is it a little unusual that she seems to aggressively hate dogs? Do you get a strange vibe from the A-level personal questions he's asking about your past? Does something feel not-quite-right about the way she forcefully grabs your arm or the fact that he told you his mother is a "big bitch"? Yeahhh. So, check please!

You spotted the red flags and got out while the getting out was good. You know what your boundaries are and you stuck to them. Good job being 'ware!

love & sex

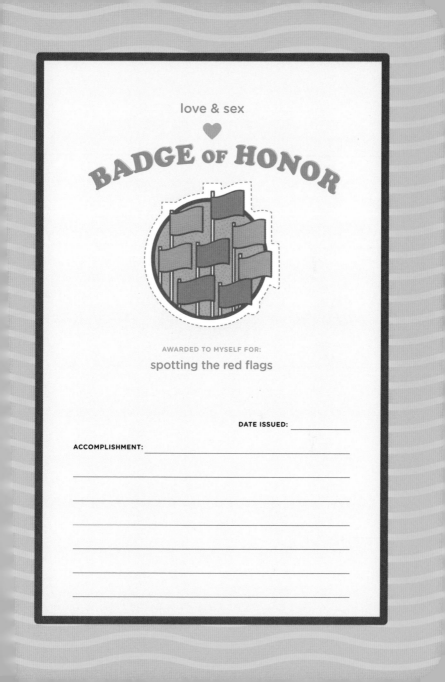

BADGE of HONOR

AWARDED TO MYSELF FOR:

spotting the red flags

DATE ISSUED: _____

ACCOMPLISHMENT: _____

_____

_____

_____

_____

_____

_____

it's not me, it's not you

Dating is incredibly stressful in practice. The stakes can feel unimaginably high. This stranger could be your last chance at love, and if they don't like you, it probably means that you're undateable. And of course, if you don't like them, they're definitely some kind of horrible monster who should be barred from engaging in social contact ever again.

Wait, none of that is true!

Just because your date is a nervous sweater, or you're taller than the other person had hoped, doesn't mean that either of you is unlovable. Someone else may *love* that he has all of *Grey's Anatomy* on DVD or that she likes to talk about how much she "hates people"! And if your date isn't into your extensive American Girl doll collection, you're not an unredeemable weirdo and they're not a jerk. You and this person aren't a match, and that is fine. Release them back into the wild, wish them the best, and let yourself off the hook. You'll live to date another day.

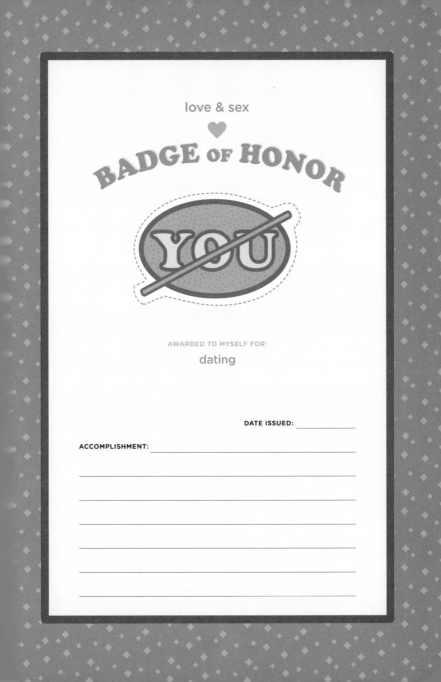

love & sex

BADGE OF HONOR

YOU

AWARDED TO MYSELF FOR:

dating

DATE ISSUED: _____

ACCOMPLISHMENT: _____

_____

_____

_____

_____

_____

_____

friends with an ex

Ending a relationship with dignity and grace is a difficult thing to do. Most people look back at their lost loves and think, "I hope that lady dies in a fire" or "I just want the best for him . . . the best spontaneous combustion of a human body ever."

But not you! You made peace with your inner teenager and are friends with an ex. You're a *real* grown-up now. You're like a Woody Allen movie. Look at you. You're a Noël Coward play. Break it down. You are very, very sophisticated, like an older, white-haired pianist who had kids with a painter, and now he lives in Paris, and it's all cool and you did a safari together last year. A++ job.

love & sex

♥

BADGE OF HONOR

BFF

AWARDED TO MYSELF FOR:

being friends with an ex

DATE ISSUED: _____

ACCOMPLISHMENT: _____

_____

_____

_____

_____

_____

_____

yes, i like that

for consent and assertiveness in bed

When you're getting biblical with another human person, you let them know exactly what you like and how you like it. This serves two purposes: 1) getting what you want and 2) letting your partner know yup, this is all aboveboard under the sheets.

Knowing you're on the same page means everyone is having fun! Communication might feel awkward or unusual at first, but knowing your partner's boundaries is sexy. It can even lead to the discovery of the kind of mutual interests you don't want to surprise someone with, but could very much still enjoy. An affirmative yes is undeniably validating for everyone involved, and a clear and unforced no saves you both from a horrible alternative. You lay it all out, and then you get laid! Win-win-win!

love & sex

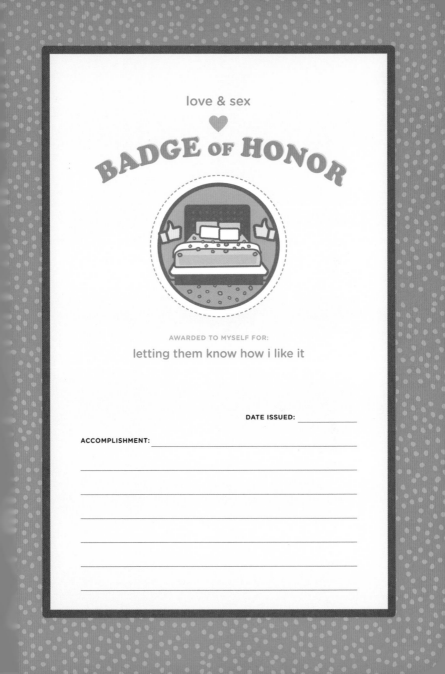

BADGE OF HONOR

AWARDED TO MYSELF FOR:

letting them know how i like it

DATE ISSUED: _____

ACCOMPLISHMENT: _____

_____

_____

_____

_____

_____

_____

what to expect when you're expecting to pee on a stick

Whether it's a joyous occasion or a gut-wrenching morning-after, your first (or your thirtieth) time peeing on a tiny stick is a formative experience in a woman's life. How often does your future hinge on urine?

To the women who approach this experience hoping for the miracle of life, who maybe have an excited partner or their own Rupert Everett at their side, we say: Good luck! Who'd make a better mama than you? Go pop them out and raise the hell out of them!

To the women whose time chugging plastic glass after plastic glass of tap water is filled with an emotion closer to dread, we say: Good luck! There is such a thing as a false positive, you know.

Either way, we drink a glass of lukewarm sink water in your honor, and award you this badge.

! ! ! !

love & sex

BADGE OF HONOR

AWARDED TO MYSELF FOR:

peeing on a stick

DATE ISSUED: _____

ACCOMPLISHMENT: _____

_____

_____

_____

_____

_____

_____

THE
plays well with others
BADGE

While it's nice to be a fully realized individual, team-work is a *Necessary Life Skill*. It can be tempting to jump to extremes in multiplayer situations—either by becoming domineering or laying down and surrendering all sense of self. There are so many ways to fail in a group (bossy, whiny, lazy, grumpy, sleepy, Doc), and one weak link can send a whole project/friendgroup/wedding party into a tailspin. A true Grown-Ass Woman makes her opinions heard, but lets her willingness to compromise prevail. You are helpful, assertive, respectful, and smart, and we would choose you as team captain any day.

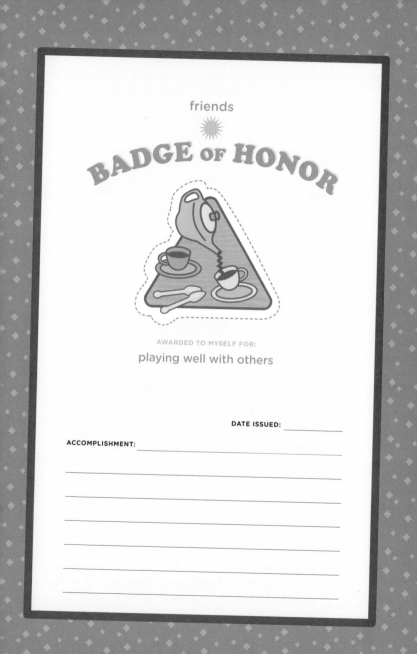

friends

BADGE OF HONOR

AWARDED TO MYSELF FOR:

playing well with others

DATE ISSUED: _____

ACCOMPLISHMENT: _____

_____

_____

_____

_____

_____

_____

THE
giver
BADGE

Whether it's the concert tickets that bring a tear to your aunt's eye, or the earrings your roommate had her eye on, or the Sharper Image/Brookstone/Sky-Mall golf gadget that your father will spend twenty minutes excitedly explaining to you, you make every present-opening experience a rewarding one. Even if you don't nail it (it turned out your girlfriend actually wanted that Vitamix you thought she was just joking about), with you it really *is* the thought that counts because the thought is there (and she loves the gloves you got her . . . her hands *are* always cold). You think hard about the people you love when you give them gifts, and you put in the effort to make them happy. It's all just one more way in which you're thoughtful and smart and generous, so keep that stuff up.

friends

BADGE OF HONOR

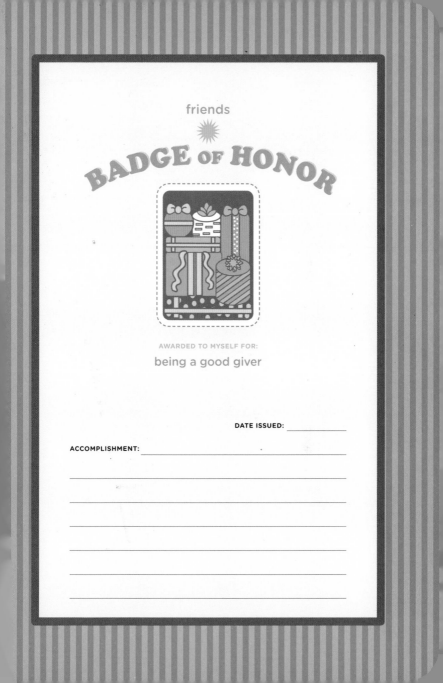

AWARDED TO MYSELF FOR:

being a good giver

DATE ISSUED: _____

ACCOMPLISHMENT: _____

_____

_____

_____

_____

_____

_____

THE
hallmark
BADGE

People love mail. Well, people hate bills, bank statements, menus, pleas for funds from various worthy places, catalogs you never signed up for, and the piles and piles and piles of flyers addressed to Resident that fall on your building's floor and never get picked up.

But people love cards! And you're an expert: birthdays, thank you notes (so key), congratulations, or holiday cards. You're enough of an adult to take the time to purchase adorable papers, handwrite a message (with your hands!), buy stamps (UGH, stamps!), look up addresses, and go to the actual mailbox. Some of you will even hand *make* beautiful little cutouts with stickers and sparkles and the works. Cards are the most heartwarming use of paper stock possible, and you have those warm hearts on lockdown.

friends

BADGE OF HONOR

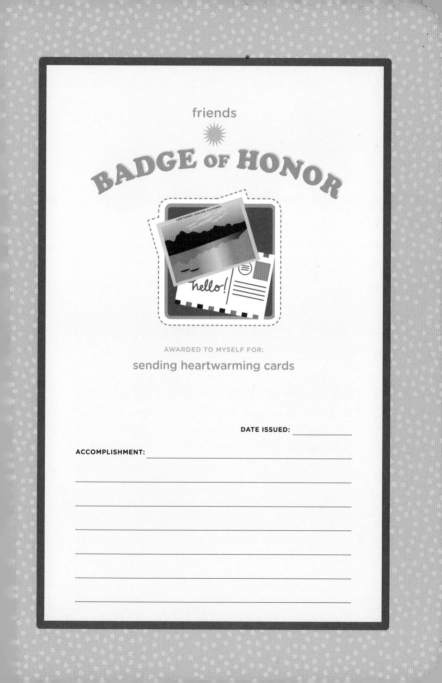

AWARDED TO MYSELF FOR:

sending heartwarming cards

DATE ISSUED: _____

ACCOMPLISHMENT: _____

_____

_____

_____

_____

_____

_____

THE
mostest
BADGE

Man, that was a great party. I mean, really great, not like, "didn't run out of alcohol, no one got punched" great. You threw a fun, interesting gathering where your guests met new people, laughed, talked, ate and drank, *and* no one threw up in your bed! That's because you did more than buy a sleeve of Solo cups and lay down a tarp. You planned and facilitated! You made introductions, refilled glasses, bought classy alcohols, and most importantly: you had fun yourself.

friends

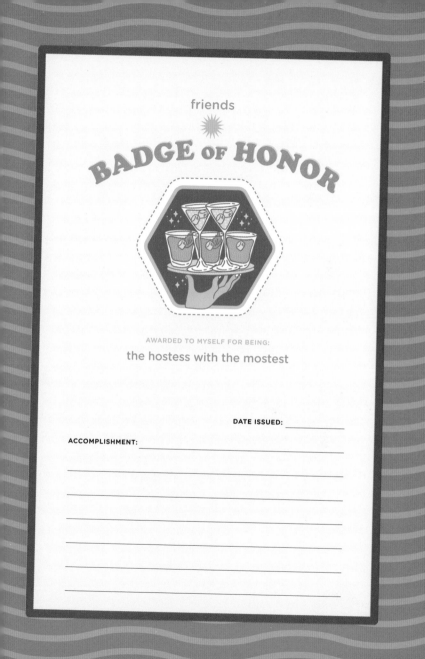

BADGE of HONOR

AWARDED TO MYSELF FOR BEING:

the hostess with the mostest

DATE ISSUED: _____

ACCOMPLISHMENT: _____

_____

_____

_____

_____

_____

_____

THE
listen up
BADGE

Maybe you give excellent advice, or maybe you just give excellent sympathetic ear. When the people in your life need someone to talk to about the issues in theirs, you're a leading choice. You have a different perspective on other people's problems or you're at least patient and kind. You cheer, comfort, or cajole them into being their best selves! People feel better after talking to you.

But whatever kind of listener you are, it doesn't go unnoticed (at least not by us). Often when people are specifically wrapped up in their own problems, they don't think about the person they're spilling those problems to. It can be exhausting and boring and just a whole lot of emotional labor, but you do it with a smile—or at least an empathetic grimace. Your effort is appreciated, ya heard?

friends

BADGE of HONOR

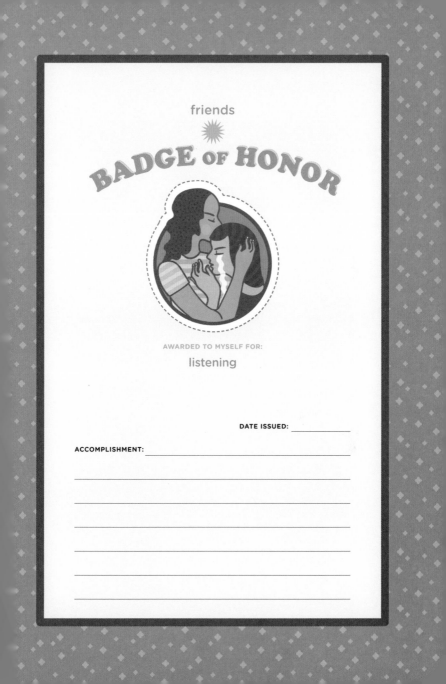

AWARDED TO MYSELF FOR:

listening

DATE ISSUED: _____

ACCOMPLISHMENT: _____

_____

_____

_____

_____

_____

_____

bitching is bonding

Sometimes trading information and even, yes, straight up talking shit can bring two people together. Whether it's commiserating with a co-worker about your unreasonable boss or relating to a fellow bridesmaid about an out-of-control maid of honor, bitching isn't just for bitches (but hey, bitches are great).

Venting is an important part of being able to handle your challenges; it's not good to let your emotions fester. Plus when you compare the sin of complaining with the sin of punching your sister in the mouth because you've been sitting on your emotions too long, venting is the clear winner. It's still important to make sure you're not dragging your friends and family down, or that you're not making your own agitation worse by fixating on it, but give yourself a little break when it comes to legitimate grievances. Your bitching buddy might be delighted to learn they're not alone.

Share this badge with the woman who knows exactly what you mean when you say, "And that noise he makes with his mouth!" She knows.

friends

BADGE of HONOR

AWARDED TO MYSELF FOR:

venting with my gal-pal

DATE ISSUED: _____

ACCOMPLISHMENT: _____

_____

_____

_____

_____

_____

_____

THE
thank you for being a friend
BADGE

This badge is for being a ridiculously amazing friend. Friendship is a lot of work: the listening, the supporting, the advising, the snapping-them-out-of-it, the commiserating, the celebrating, the partying, the inside-joking, the birthday-remembering, the hanging out, the laughing, the laughing, the laughing, and allllllllllllll of the baby-doll-pajama pillow fights (they're real, boys). Whether you are connected by family ties, the bonds of friendship, or just the little wires floating in outer space that make up the internet, your always-open door and always-open self are deeply appreciated.

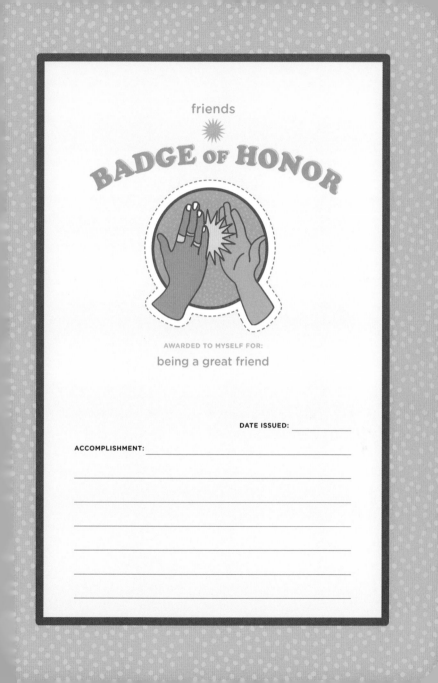

friends

BADGE OF HONOR

AWARDED TO MYSELF FOR:

being a great friend

DATE ISSUED: _____

ACCOMPLISHMENT: _____

_____

_____

_____

_____

_____

_____

pretending to be happy for someone

"You were just *pretending* to be happy for me," is one of the most cutting things a rom-com best friend can say to the heroine at the movie's emotional climax. But as a Grown-Ass Woman, you know that pretending to be happy for people is key to being a pleasant, functional adult. Plus, it's the first step toward summoning the real happiness you don't yet feel.

When your friend gets engaged to a guy who makes you think, "Oh wow, they are doing this," you say, "Oh! Wow! You! Are! Doing! This!" and make it sound like real enthusiasm. You act excited for the cousin who's having a baby with the boyfriend she swore she was about to break up with. You can even dredge up graciousness when your colleague gets a bonus you were gunning for, instead of doing what's in your heart and yelling, "NOT. FAIR."

Even if you're totally faking your grin, you don't rain on anyone else's parade. And that kind of good behavior deserves a parade of its own!

friends

BADGE OF HONOR

AWARDED TO MYSELF FOR:

pretending to be happy for someone else

DATE ISSUED: _____

ACCOMPLISHMENT: _____

_____

_____

_____

_____

_____

_____

boundaries

Adults have different relationships that serve different functions. Sometimes, those lines can get blurred and complications ensue. That is why psychology invented boundaries! This might mean not getting sloppy drunk with your co-workers, or not hitting on your doctor, or even just not telling the bagel guy about your yeast infection (even though he works with yeast). It might mean not napping in your roommate's bed or calling your friend's mom just to chat. Grown-Ass Women recognize that you can't let your guard down around everyone all of the time, and that people need people . . . but they also need space.

investment

Okay so you get money, you have the money, now what? For you, it's not hiding the cash in your mattress, or spending it all and waiting for your next check—it's investing.

Important secret: Rich people don't just get rich from high-paying jobs and inherited wealth (although that helps), they make their money work for them, instead of spending it all on Seamless. And so do you.

When you look at the stock exchange, you don't see meaningless letters and confusing numbers and oh, so many arrows (what is with all the arrows??), you see opportunity. Maybe you've done the thoughtful research and you know what a bond is and when a stock pays dividends and when to say "BUY!" and when to scream "SELL!" and why they ding that bell every day.

Go take your dollars and turn them into more dollars like a damn magician.

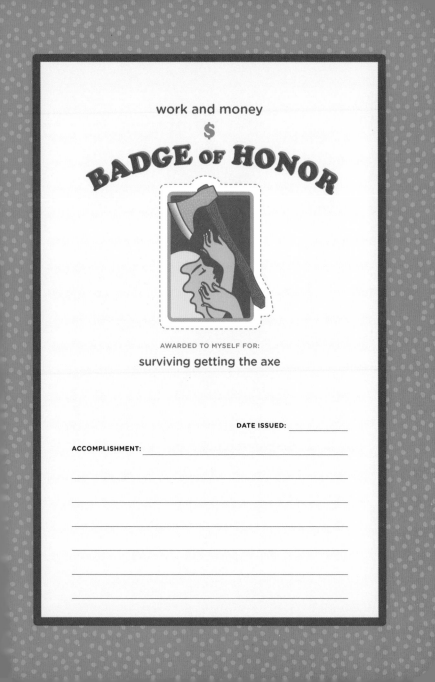

THE
axed
BADGE

Maybe it was a layoff, maybe it was a company collapse, or maybe you got your ass fired: the problem is you're now unemployed. Any of the above can happen to the best of us, but despite how common it is, the loss of a job can be terrifying. Your continued survival is the badge-winner here: keeping positive in the face of adworsity, keeping the hunt alive, and *not* making those pajamas your uniform or becoming dependent on your psychic friend.

Eventually, you'll get back on your feet and start high-achieving all over the place. And when you're at your next job and some young kid asks you for advice, you can tell them about how you bounced back, how you never gave up, how you found the right job for you and made it your own.

Oprah was fired from a TV station in Baltimore. Never forget that.

work and money

$

BADGE of HONOR

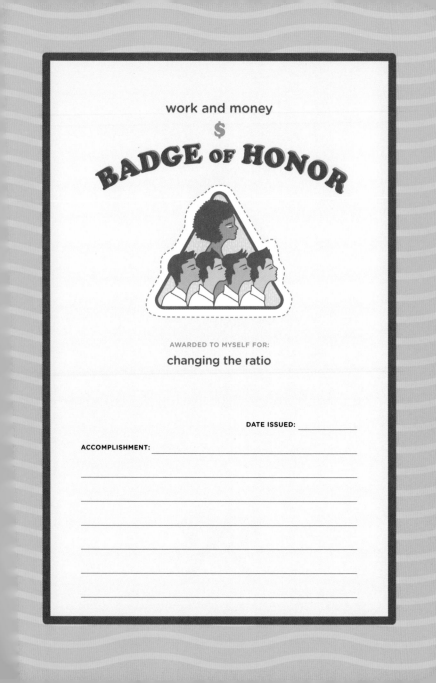

AWARDED TO MYSELF FOR:

changing the ratio

DATE ISSUED: _____

ACCOMPLISHMENT: _____

_____

_____

_____

_____

_____

_____

changing the ratio

Fun fact: A lot of industries, from tech to comedy to truck driving, are dispiritingly male-dominated. But you already know that because you're a woman dealing with a room full of men.

Making your way into the boys club is a big deal—you always have to be better, smarter, stronger, and faster (okay, maybe not faster) than the dudes. But we need women like you: in the lab, in the improv class, on the long haul. You're walking/talking proof that women can do anything men can do, which we all knew, but they might not have.

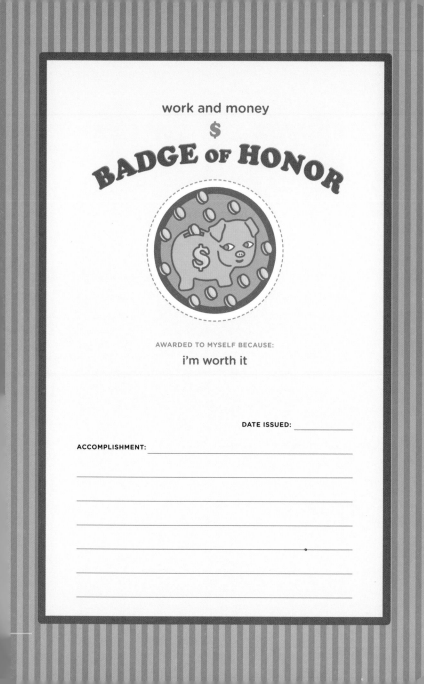

work and money

$

BADGE OF HONOR

AWARDED TO MYSELF BECAUSE:

i'm worth it

DATE ISSUED: _____

ACCOMPLISHMENT: _____

_____

_____

_____

_____

_____

_____

THE
i'm worth it
BADGE

We've all heard that women are less likely to ask for and receive a raise than their male counterparts. This is ridiculous and also, duh, because of EVERY-THING WE'VE EVER BEEN TAUGHT! But you took this national problem and created a personal solution: you asked for that raise.

It's hard to ask for more cash; it's awkward and intimidating and didn't your grandmother tell you never to talk about money? Just kidding, she said, "GET PAID." You like seeing that extra cash in the bank and knowing you went after what is rightfully yours. Looking objectively at your worth and realizing how valuable you are is a brave and impressive thing. You deserve it!

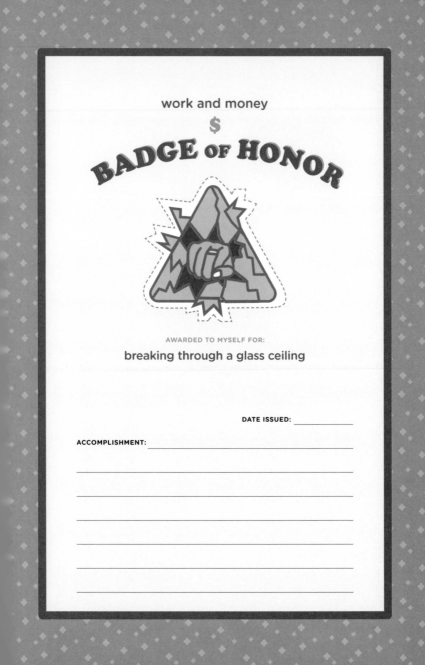

work and money

$

BADGE OF HONOR

AWARDED TO MYSELF FOR:

breaking through a glass ceiling

DATE ISSUED: _____

ACCOMPLISHMENT: _____

_____

_____

_____

_____

_____

_____

glass ceiling

Oh my God, are you okay?!? There are shards of glass everywhere, but somehow you seem strangely unharmed. Ohhh, that's just that glass ceiling you broke. Nicely done.

You are going for it, whatever "it" is for you — a promotion, a new job, a better desk, whatever. You may be a nice person, but you want to be a nice person with a corner office, or a nice person with your name in lights, or a nice person with all the successes and accolades you so richly deserve. Ambition is a beautiful thing when done well, and necessary to being the baddest bitch possible. Too frequently, assertive women are called bitches *in the bad sense* (why is there even a bad sense?), but we know that you are a lady who knows what she wants and gets what she wants, and that deserves a badge.

friend's engagement even if you believe it is ill-fated? That is something to celebrate! Paid all your bills on time? Hell yeah you did, here's a badge!

Being a full-grown, independent woman means a lot of things, but mostly it means being your own cheerleader. While your friends, family, and significant others love you, it's important to be in your own corner, and in these pages you can celebrate every work success, family kindness, and unforgettable milestone that make you the cool, self-sufficient lady you are.

Go forth and live your life, and be shocked and amazed by how many badges you earn every day. The Grown-Ass Women's Club wants you as a member.

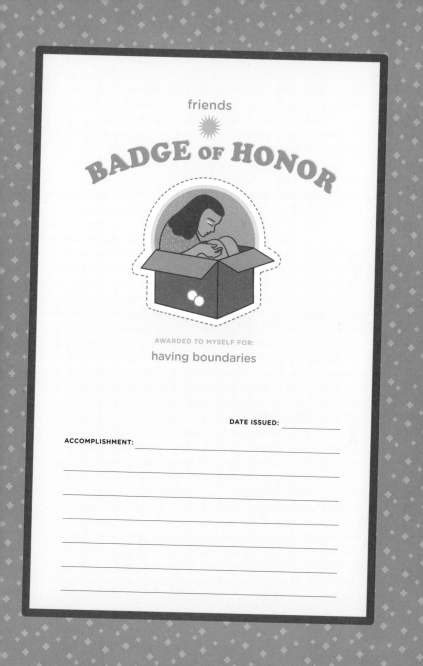

friends

BADGE OF HONOR

AWARDED TO MYSELF FOR:

having boundaries

DATE ISSUED: _____

ACCOMPLISHMENT: _____

_____

_____

_____

_____

_____

_____

THE
gyno you don't want to but you did
BADGE

Is it low-grade insulting that women need a whole separate doctor to keep their innards in tip-top shape while dudes can go to any GP, turn their heads, and cough? Kind of! Does anyone enjoy the feeling of cold stirrups and the scent of stale exam room air? Is it fun to sit in a waiting room watching soap operas while you consider the ramifications of a year's worth of choices and read articles about biological clocks until you can hear everyone in the room's ticking? Resounding no! But it is all necessary and important. This badge is for going to your yearly gynecological appointment. Whether she okayed you for your second kid or told you that you have a touch of gonorrhea, you went. Good for you. And hey, you look great in that gown.

upkeep

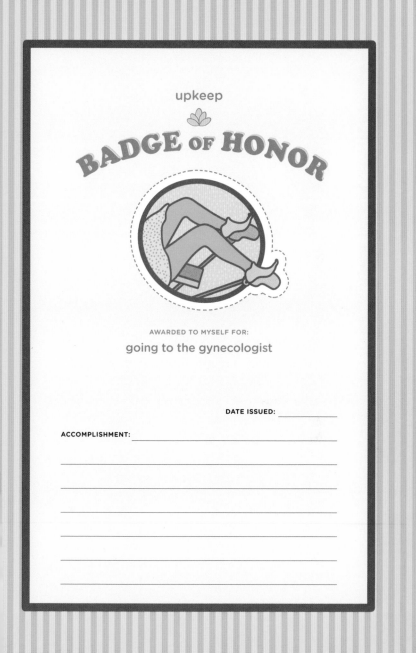

BADGE OF HONOR

AWARDED TO MYSELF FOR:

going to the gynecologist

DATE ISSUED: _____

ACCOMPLISHMENT: _____

_____

_____

_____

_____

_____

_____

makeup removal

It's been a long day and you're tired, and you want to go right to bed. But not before making a quick pit stop in the bathroom: to remove your makeup the way God and *Cosmo* have long told us we should. Before you zonk out, you faithfully remove your eyeliner and wipe off Kylie's lip kit, so you can drift off to sleep as fresh faced as an Amish teenager.

Even though wearing yesterday's eyeliner gives you that Courtney Love glow, you know that treating your skin well is important, since it will hopefully be with you a long time. Like, the whole time. Like, until full body skin-transplants become a super normal thing that all the *Real Housewives* are doing. But even then, you'll be wearing your own skin, because you take such good care of it now.

upkeep

BADGE OF HONOR

AWARDED TO MYSELF FOR:

managing to remove my makeup

DATE ISSUED: _____

ACCOMPLISHMENT: _____

_____

_____

_____

_____

_____

_____

gym class hero

It turns out those inspirational Nike commercials were right: exercise can make you feel pretty damn good. As we get older, it's more vital than ever to move our bodies, which are sinking into the abyss of old age, and you know that bed-to-couch-to-fridge-to-bed routine is not quite enough. Swimming, climbing, barre class, spin class, CrossFit, dancing like no one's watching in your own room—whatever it is, you've figured out an exercise plan that works for you. Whether you're one of those enviable people who just "don't feel like themselves" unless they've gotten a run in, or you're hiding in the back of yoga hoping no one notices that your Warrior II is more of a Warrior I and a half, you put in the effort and get the exercise you need. You, as they say, just did it!

upkeep

BADGE OF HONOR

AWARDED TO MYSELF FOR:

getting the exercise i need

DATE ISSUED: _____

ACCOMPLISHMENT: _____

_____

_____

_____

_____

_____

_____

dry clean only

Honestly, why are so many things dry clean only? You can't even go to an H&M without accidentally buying a top that comes with a secret maintenance tax. But this doesn't bother you (or at least doesn't bother you much) because you take care of your clothing the way it wants to be taken care of.

You don't shove cashmere in with your other laundry and hope the washer doesn't shrink it. You don't throw silk in a bag that somehow always remains in the corner of your closet and never quite makes it to the friendly, overpriced place around the corner. You hand wash your hand washables, you press your button-down shirts, and you never wring *anything* out in that certain way you're not supposed to that stretches and ruins every single kind of fabric. You show up to work and other events looking pressed and polished, fresh off of whatever it is dry cleaners do to clothing (blow on it?). You look sharp, keep it up.

upkeep

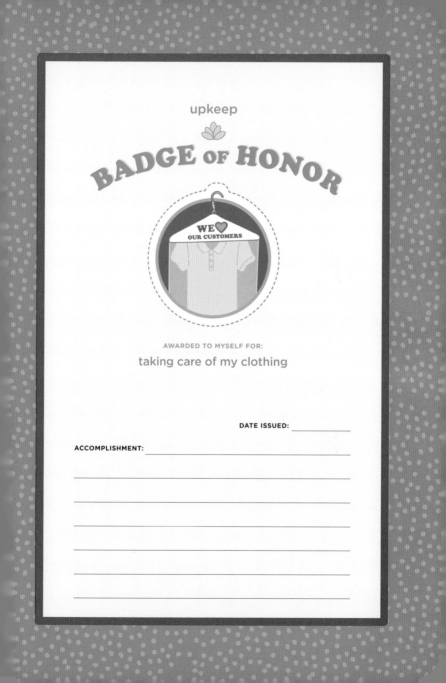

BADGE OF HONOR

WE ♥
OUR CUSTOMERS

AWARDED TO MYSELF FOR:

taking care of my clothing

DATE ISSUED: _____

ACCOMPLISHMENT: _____

_____

_____

_____

_____

_____

_____

a crow is afoot

What is that on your face? Is it . . . pen? Is it a chenille mark? Did you go to a club where the handstamp was an almost-imperceptible line, and then fall asleep on your hand so that the stamp transferred onto your face? No. It's your very first wrinkle, congratulations and welcome.

We (rightfully) make a big deal out of milestones like a young woman's first period or twenty-first birthday, but we never celebrate the step into true womanhood that is the appearance of the first wrinkle. Your previously unseen wisdom is becoming visible, and this is the first warning sign that slowly, over years, men are going to stop being weird at you the way they are now, and be weird at you in a whole new way. This is your first step to becoming a cool old broad who yells at teens and wears caftans, so embrace it. You're going to be a great elder stateswoman, and it's starting to show.

upkeep

BADGE OF HONOR

AWARDED TO MYSELF FOR:

getting my first wrinkle

DATE ISSUED: _____

ACCOMPLISHMENT: _____

_____

_____

_____

_____

_____

_____

presentable home

Quick, someone important is coming over to your apartment right now—how ready are you? If you're frantically throwing stray pants into your bathroom closet and pushing takeout containers further underneath the bed: bless you, we've all been there!

But if you're smiling serenely and straightening an already-fluffed throw pillow, this badge is for you. Keeping your home—be it apartment, house, or SRO—baseline clean is a true mark of grownness. Relax on your already-tidy couch, with no pizza boxes to push out of the way.

home life

BADGE OF HONOR

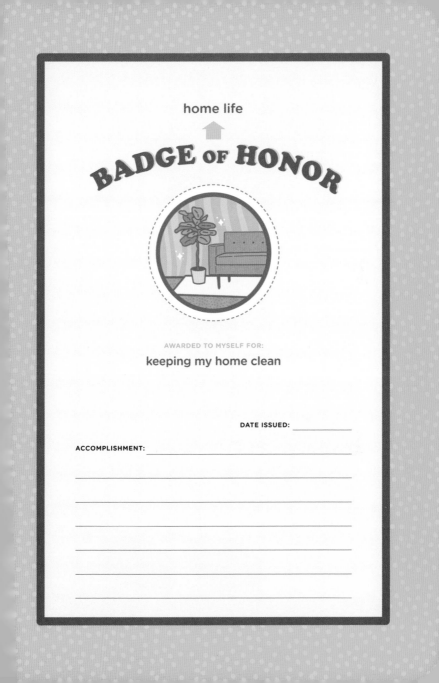

AWARDED TO MYSELF FOR:

keeping my home clean

DATE ISSUED: _____

ACCOMPLISHMENT: _____

_____

_____

_____

_____

_____

_____

THE
rent is too damn high
BADGE

"It's such a nice neighborhood!" You said. "There's a FOUNTAIN in the LOBBY!" You protested. "There's a doorman, and he calls me, 'Miss'!" You insisted. And then you looked at your bank account. And then you looked at your life, and you also gave a passing glance at your choices. And then you got realistic and you picked a home or apartment that was within your means.

Now your neighborhood is a little less nice than you might have dreamed. The only water running in your lobby is a leaky pipe, and the man outside your door who calls you "Miss" when you return home is not employed by your landlord (although he claims he's on a mission from God, so that's promising). Yeah, you live in a shithole, but this is what it means to be on your own! Your place is yours, and no one can take that away from you, because you pay for it. Pour us a glass of brown tap water and we'll toast to you!

home life

BADGE OF HONOR

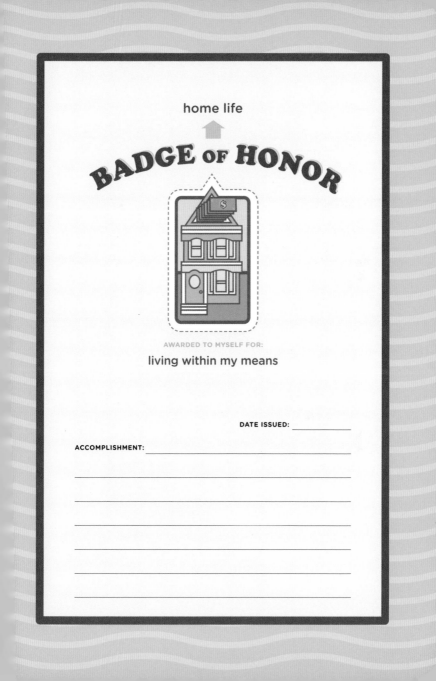

AWARDED TO MYSELF FOR:

living within my means

DATE ISSUED: _____

ACCOMPLISHMENT: _____

_____

_____

_____

_____

_____

_____

you made your bed

You know what only grown-ups have and small children or broke college students or post-collegiate stragglers don't? A really nice bed. Okay, fine, sometimes small children have really nice beds (the race-car ones are pretty solid, TBH), but it's not like they *paid* for them.

Maybe it's a fancy body-adhering mattress, or maybe it's eleven million thread count sheets, or maybe it's enough pillows to comfortably lend your bed to a hydra—you put some thought into the place where you rest your head. When you're tucking yourself in tonight, remember how it felt to sleep in that dorm room single or on those Lego sheets, and count your successes.

home life

BADGE OF HONOR

AWARDED TO MYSELF FOR:

making a comfortable bed

DATE ISSUED: _____

ACCOMPLISHMENT: _____

_____

_____

_____

_____

_____

_____

cohabitation

Living with your significant other is an impressive thing. Not only are you dealing with all of their business, all of yours is on display, too. Massive diarrhea? He's right on the other side of that bathroom door. The recurring nightmare that causes you to sleepwalk to the kitchen? She's the one guiding you back to bed. If you want to spend all of Saturday yelling at *Bar Rescue* and drinking hot toddies in your caftan, that person is there, seeing the realest you (and if you're lucky, boiling water for another round). You do the work to make your house a home. To the brave, who wake up every day to a faceful of morning breath, you deserve a round of applause. *And* so does the lovely person picking your wet towels up off the bathroom floor.

home life

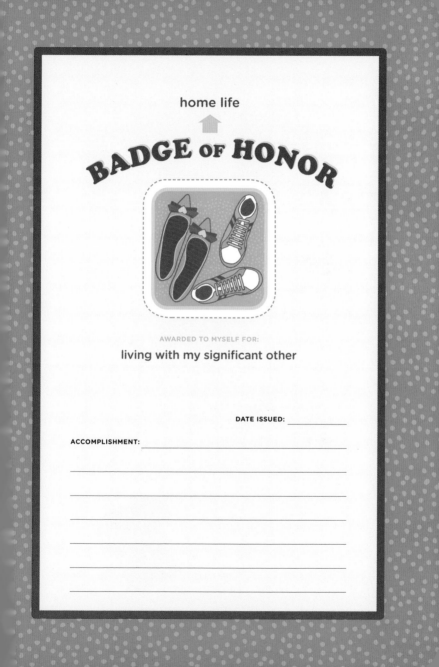

BADGE OF HONOR

AWARDED TO MYSELF FOR:

living with my significant other

DATE ISSUED: _____

ACCOMPLISHMENT: _____

_____

_____

_____

_____

_____

_____

closet clean out

Marie Kondo is an adorable woman with some charming ideas, but the premise that you can clean out your home one time over a period of a year and then you're done for the rest of your life is bonkers. In this age of fast fashion and rabid consumption and you know, stuff, many people find themselves doing a closet clean out a couple of times a year, at least. And it's *never easy*! For all the time you didn't get bogged down in old yearbooks (and all the time you did—can you believe Mark Conners had the nerve to write what he did after you helped him so much in Chem?), for all the cerulean corduroys that somehow survived the last purge, for that one necklace from an ex you can't bear to throw out even though it resolutely *does not spark joy*—you got through the closet purge because you know it's good for you. Don't you feel lighter?

home life

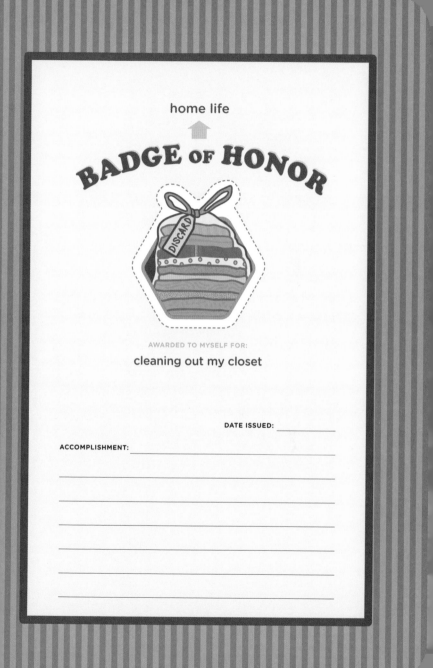

BADGE OF HONOR

AWARDED TO MYSELF FOR:

cleaning out my closet

DATE ISSUED: _____

ACCOMPLISHMENT: _____

_____

_____

_____

_____

_____

_____

good houseguest

Staying with friends, family, or Airbnb strangers can be a nice way to save money and spend time with people you care about and/or don't know at all. It can also be a nice way to burn some freaking bridges, if you're not careful.

You're a good houseguest because you know the important, unwritten houseguest bylaws about boundaries, graciousness, and when to leave. You don't eat all the food in the house or take two-hour showers. You bring a thank-you gift and send a note. You leave your bed nicer than you found it. You don't loudly watch TV all night, invite unexpected extra guests, or make unreasonable demands on your host's time.

home life

BADGE OF HONOR

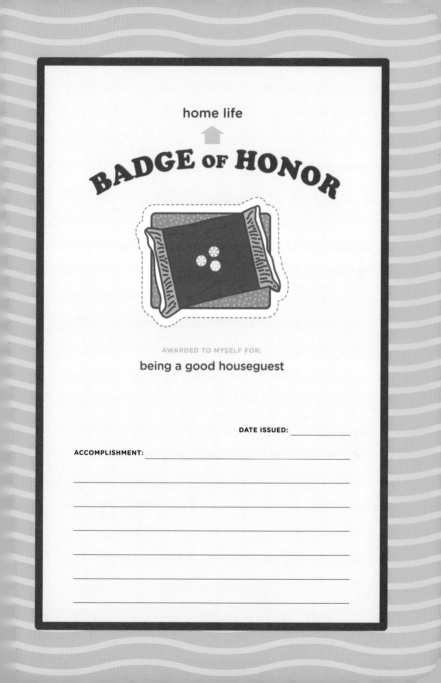

AWARDED TO MYSELF FOR:

being a good houseguest

DATE ISSUED: _____

ACCOMPLISHMENT: _____

_____

_____

_____

_____

_____

_____

i'm not that kid anymore!

Families can be, in a funny way, like middle school. Some small, forgettable act, embarrassing moment, or three-year-long sullen phase can get you a reputation for *life*. Whether you went from angsty goth teen to sunny, Lululemon–wearing grown-up—or even from sandbox-hogging child to a soup kitchen–volunteering adult—it can be hard to shake the image your parents, siblings, and extended family have of you. How can you convince them you've changed?

There are two answers to that question: 1) through patience, self-assurance, and consistently behaving like the person you've become or 2) you can't. Yup, often, you just can't! Relatives don't always accept change, even positive change, easily—there's comfort in the familiar, and you can't spell "family" without "familiar" (plus a "y," minus some other letters). But just because your family sees you as a person you haven't been for years, that doesn't mean that you should revert to past behavior to fulfill other people's expectations. Keep being the person you know you are, and forgive your family for missing the old you.

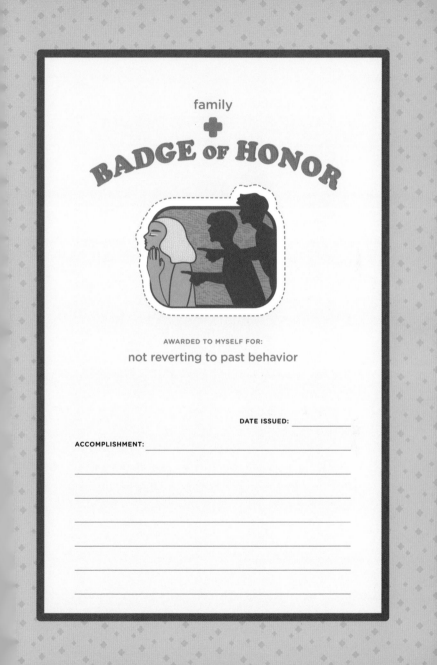

family

✚

BADGE OF HONOR

AWARDED TO MYSELF FOR:

not reverting to past behavior

DATE ISSUED: _____

ACCOMPLISHMENT: _____

_____

_____

_____

_____

_____

_____

finding common ground with mom

You're a Grown-Ass Woman now, and you know who else is a Grown-Ass Woman? Your mom!

You're not a tiny baby or a bratty teenager. You're an adult with adult interests and adult opinions. Math and logic indicate that your mom probably is too! Maybe you both love racquetball, or baking bread, or Johnny Cash, or making snarky jokes about the people in your hometown.

All of your family members are, believe it or not, full and complete people outside of whatever role they play in your life. If you take the time to learn more about who that person is, you might just have a new friend.

So ask your mom about her hobbies, her favorite TV shows, her friends, or her thoughts on the best way to make paella. It's nice to have more in common with the woman who raised you than being the only two people who know that when you met Cinderella, you were so excited you peed. Give yourself some new, drier memories.

family

BADGE of HONOR

AWARDED TO MYSELF FOR:

finding common ground with mom

DATE ISSUED: _____

ACCOMPLISHMENT: _____

_____

_____

_____

_____

_____

_____

THE
nightingale
BADGE

Whether it's for a dirt mogul–jumping husband, an ill parent, or just a whiny roommate with a cold, the level of care that you provide the downtrodden and weak will go on your permanent record in the "plus" column.

The stereotype that all women are nurturing isn't actually true. Taking care of others isn't a thing that comes easily to all people, and dealing with everything from the sniffles to the heartaches that come with a loved one being out of commission takes a lot of fortitude. This isn't about being women, this is about being Grown Ass: taking responsibility for the well-being of another.

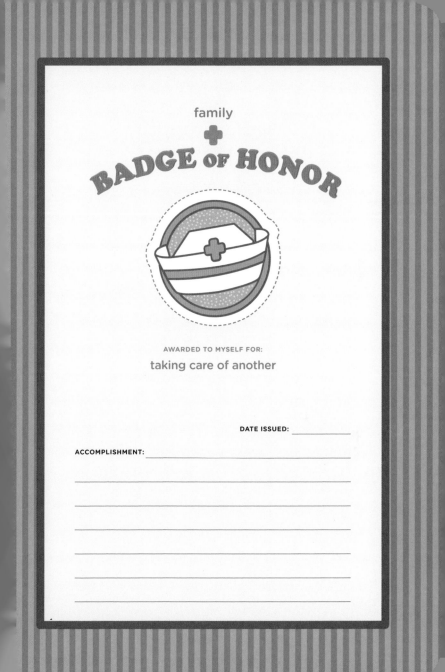

family

✚

BADGE of HONOR

AWARDED TO MYSELF FOR:

taking care of another

DATE ISSUED: _____

ACCOMPLISHMENT: _____

_____

_____

_____

_____

_____

_____

medical report

As we age, so do our parents. And as our parents age, so do their friends and neighbors. For every time you've called your family, only to be regaled with a long list of the ailments of loved ones and relative strangers, this badge is for you.

But it's not just gross and depressing health stuff: for every time you've picked up the phone and had the progress of the kitchen remodel painstakingly explained to you, you're making someone's day. Every time you listen to the saga of your mother's coworker's niece's custody dispute, you're doing a mitzvah.

Kudos to you for understanding that these things are newsworthy to your loved one and that by sharing the details with you, they are trying to connect. Here are some key phrases to repeat as necessary: "Oh, I'm sorry to hear that." "Wow, taking care of your heart IS important." "Dry rot? It's always something!" "Well, you really never know, do you?"

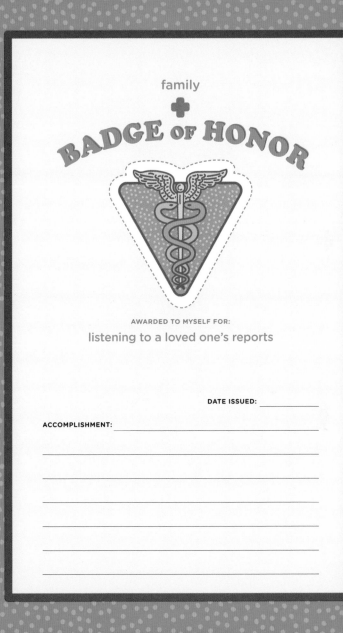

family

BADGE OF HONOR

AWARDED TO MYSELF FOR:

listening to a loved one's reports

DATE ISSUED: _____

ACCOMPLISHMENT: _____

_____

_____

_____

_____

_____

_____

personal style

Maybe your style icon is Annie Potts in *Pretty in Pink*, or Solange Knowles, or Grace Kelly, or your older cousin Melanie who has *such great bangs* and impeccable handbags. But our style icon is you, because you have such a great, original look.

This badge is for covering yourself, or barely covering yourself, in fabulous pieces that are truly you. Maybe expressing yourself *requires* zebra print, tulle, colored tights, leather shorts, and wacky art-teacher earrings. Maybe it means a subdued pencil skirt and the perfect Mansur sandals. Whatever your style, it's no accident. You know which sweater will make your eyes pop, what leather jacket will straddle the line between tough and chic, and which heels will remind everyone how dope your legs are. Whether you shop at Gucci or exclusively at thrift stores, what's most important is that you look like YOU. You make looking good look good.

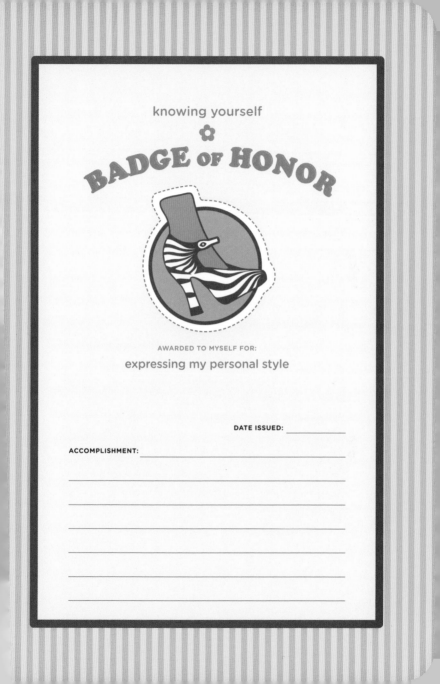

knowing yourself

❀

BADGE OF HONOR

AWARDED TO MYSELF FOR:

expressing my personal style

DATE ISSUED: _____

ACCOMPLISHMENT: _____

_____

_____

_____

_____

_____

_____

unapologetic romcom watcher

The idea that there is such a thing as a "guilty" pleasure needs to die. First of all, what pleasure is there in guilt? Very little! Pleasure usually comes from allowing yourself joy without the guilt—whether it's a romantic comedy addiction, a lifelong need for pop music, or a serious dependency on reality TV. These things are created to be enjoyed.

That's why you don't whisper that you're going to re-re-re-re-rewatch *Definitely, Maybe* (a *definitely, not maybe* underrated *romcom*). And you don't only listen to Carly Rae Jepsen alone in your car (although you do there, too). You host un-ironic *Real Housewives* reunion parties; you carry *Us Weekly* proudly from the mailbox instead of hiding it under your junk mail. You don't let anyone tell you that the thing you like to watch/hear/read is less than. Life is too short.

Now, turn up this Britney song, it's the best.

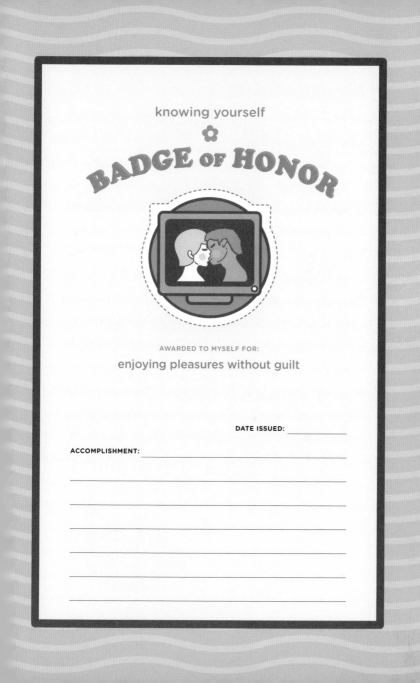

knowing yourself

✿

BADGE of HONOR

AWARDED TO MYSELF FOR:

enjoying pleasures without guilt

DATE ISSUED: _____

ACCOMPLISHMENT: _____

_____

_____

_____

_____

_____

_____

not tonight

When you go to a party, you *go to a party*. You're plenty of fun. But sometimes you don't go to a party. You just don't. And that's okay too.

It can be unspeakably nice to just opt out once in a while. Maybe you curl up on your own home couch and finally watch that eight-hour O.J. documentary, or whatever Freeform has On Demand. Maybe you take a long bath with a sheet mask, maybe you read that book you've been meaning to get to, maybe you order fried chicken sandwiches.

Declining an invitation to a fun evening doesn't mean you're missing everything! All it means is that you're getting some quality time for you: time to relax, time to recharge, time to be quiet, and time to read or watch or do the fun and interesting things that make you a better party guest.

knowing yourself

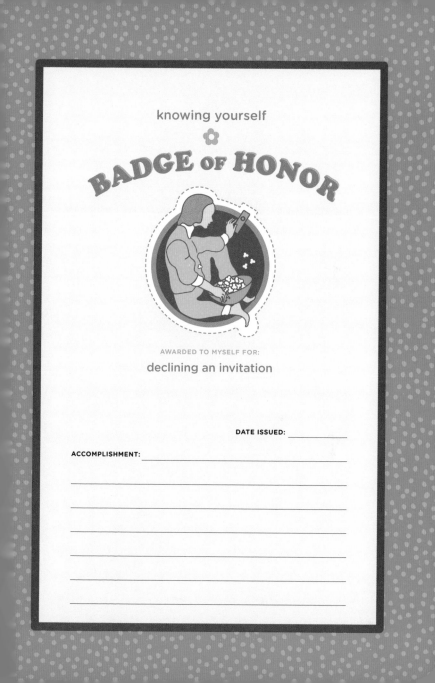

BADGE OF HONOR

AWARDED TO MYSELF FOR:

declining an invitation

DATE ISSUED: _____

ACCOMPLISHMENT: _____

_____

_____

_____

_____

_____

_____

treat yo' self

Being grown means that when you're sick or sad or overwhelmed, the person most invested in making sure you feel better is you. Sure, a partner or friends or even family might care, but at the end of the day, your physical and emotional well-being is your own responsibility. This *also* means there's at least one person who can seriously spoil you: you.

This badge is for what you do just for you, as an adult of some amount of means and/or creativity. Whether it's going ahead and buying that long-lusted-after leather jacket or just taking yourself to a much needed daytime movie, you indulge you as expertly as any permissive grandparent. Of course you can't afford to do this kind of thing all the time (you don't want to raise yourself into a brat), but once in a while isn't going to hurt anyone. You deserve it.

knowing yourself

✿

BADGE OF HONOR

AWARDED TO MYSELF FOR:

spoiling myself every so often

DATE ISSUED: _____

ACCOMPLISHMENT: _____

_____

_____

_____

_____

_____

_____

talent show

It takes a lot to belt out "It's All Coming Back to Me Now" or a kickass Jewel song in front of karaoke patrons. It takes a lot to be the first person on the dance floor at a wedding. It takes a lot to get up at that open mic night and do a tight five/original ballad/accordion solo. But you're putting your performative skills out there, and you have our applause.

Instead of being rewarded with rolled eyes, or drunken boos, or the unwanted attentions of that one dude who thinks your artistic spirit means it's cool to touch you, you're rewarded with glory—even if it's in a key only you can hear. We're impressed with your talent (of course), but also your gumption, because it can be scary to show other people your moves/high notes/best jokes. The love of the crowd, or at least the high fives of your friends, is the greatest gift of all.

knowing yourself

❀

BADGE OF HONOR

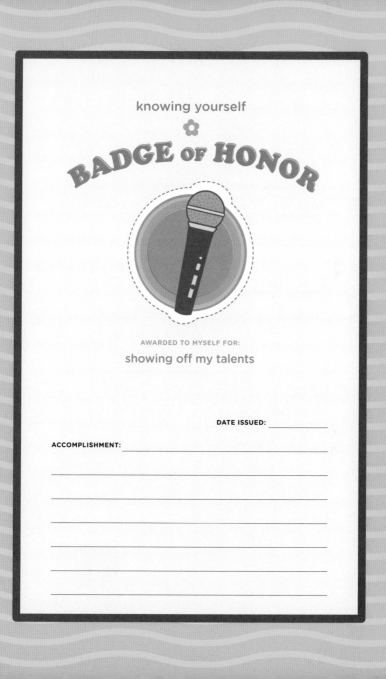

AWARDED TO MYSELF FOR:

showing off my talents

DATE ISSUED: _____

ACCOMPLISHMENT: _____

_____

_____

_____

_____

_____

_____

_____

THE
adventurer
BADGE

You may not always have the cash for that Caribbean cruise, or even that chick-from-your-office's Hamptons summer share, but you're always down for an adventure. Be it a day trip or a road trip or the three-month hiking expedition you've been planning since you were twelve, you like to put on your giant sunglasses, wrap that bandana around your head, and go. Or maybe lace up your boots, climb into that scuba gear, put on your helmet, strap on those goggles, pull on your driving gloves—whatever's necessary. The number one best way to try new stuff is to *try new stuff*.

It can be easy to do all the same stuff all the time: eat the same food, walk the same routes, climb the same mountains. But you're not satisfied with the same old, same old—you want the different new, different new! Whether it's ice-fishing in Alaska, camping in the Mojave Desert, or just trying the farther away coffee place, you're testing out the newest frontiers.

expanding your horizons

BADGE OF HONOR

AWARDED TO MYSELF FOR:

being up for adventure

DATE ISSUED: _____

ACCOMPLISHMENT: _____

_____

_____

_____

_____

_____

_____

jetsetter
for international travel

They call you Ms. Worldwide, which, I'm sorry, means you're related to Pitbull. But in a cool way! Maybe you've been all over, or maybe you just finished your first trip away from American soil. You dealt with language barriers and the impossible math of your currency to not-your-currency, and you were rewarded with amazing food, fantastic scenery, a greater understanding of the human condition, and cool souvenirs, probably. The point is, you went abroad, you fantastic broad. What'd you bring us?

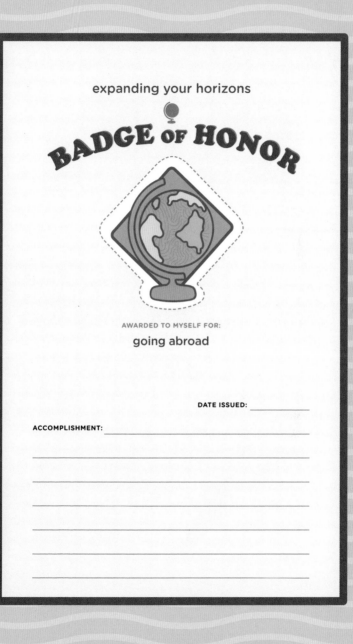

expanding your horizons

BADGE OF HONOR

AWARDED TO MYSELF FOR:

going abroad

DATE ISSUED: _____

ACCOMPLISHMENT: _____

_____

_____

_____

_____

_____

_____

hotel room for one

There are a lot of advantages to traveling with someone else. Like, you always have someone to watch your bag at the airport while you run to the bathroom. But there are some pretty huge advantages to traveling alone, too—like the time and space to get to know yourself.

Whether it's a twelve-hour jaunt to the next city or a month-long safari, you're not afraid to set out into that big world unencumbered. You can do whatever you want without worrying about anyone else's schedule, and that's the kind of freedom women just didn't have for most of human history. There's nothing quite like eating dinner in a new place all alone, as a woman of mystery. You can carry your own bags, book your own rooms, and get by in the world by your (not-so) lonesome.

expanding your horizons

BADGE OF HONOR

AWARDED TO MYSELF FOR:

traveling alone

DATE ISSUED: _____

ACCOMPLISHMENT: _____

_____

_____

_____

_____

_____

_____

drastic haircut

Changing the way your *entire head* looks is a bigger move than people really understand. Whether it's going long to short, blonde to black, or getting a brand new weave, there's a reason those girls on *Top Model* cried every Makeover Day. A lot of women cut or color to signify a change in their lives, which is wonderfully *Felicity* of them, and it's badge-worthy whether it's a new beginning or just a new look because you were bored.

You went out and got yourself a whole different head. You take no prisoners. You get this badge.

expanding your horizons

BADGE of HONOR

AWARDED TO MYSELF FOR:

getting a drastic haircut

DATE ISSUED: _____

ACCOMPLISHMENT: _____

_____

_____

_____

_____

_____

_____

reporting for duty

An envelope came in the mail. It looked official and your name was on it. What could it be? The draft? *The Hunger Games*? Your dentist? No, it's jury duty, and you reported for it.

Okay, sure, jury duty is compulsory, and maybe you only did it after stalling the maximum number of times and only then so you wouldn't go to jail or get fined or whatever happens to undutiful Americans, but STILL. It's your civic duty, and you did it. You waited in a sweaty or oddly freezing room with your fellow citizens, watched a deeply silly video about jurisprudence and your obligations as a resident of your state, and maybe you even got picked. If you did, you have the not-at-all terrifying honor of deciding another person's fate, and that's a big deal! Hey, at least you got time off work?

grown-ass citizenship

BADGE OF HONOR

AWARDED TO MYSELF FOR:

reporting for jury duty

DATE ISSUED: _____

ACCOMPLISHMENT: _____

_____

_____

_____

_____

_____

_____

THE
see something,
stand for something
BADGE

Imagine this: You're sitting on the subway or the bus, trying to wake up and listening to the same Robyn song on repeat (it's called a "morning mix," thank you), and a very old or very pregnant or very be-crutched individual gets on. What happens next? Your seat becomes their seat as you grapple for the bar or try to find a place on the pole where that lady who wiped her nose on her mitten is not touching your hands too much. You're happy knowing you did something for someone else.

Your goodwill doesn't stop at the subway doors—you're well aware that other people are trying to get by too, and you do what you can to help. Sometimes this means holding a door, or helping a woman with a stroller up the stairs, or letting the harried-looking dad with four kids take the last parking space at the mall. It's good to get yours, but it's great to make sure other people get theirs too.

grown-ass citizenship

★

BADGE of HONOR

AWARDED TO MYSELF FOR:

showing goodwill to others

DATE ISSUED: _____

ACCOMPLISHMENT: _____

_____

_____

_____

_____

_____

_____

THE
i voted
BADGE

Like you'd let a chance to speak your mind *pass you by*! Look, we've all run the numbers on how much an individual vote counts and it looks bleak, but it's actually important!

I don't know if you know this, but you can vote in *local elections*, not just national ones. And in local elections, you're voting for the people who deal with stuff that affects your day-to-day life, like what gun and abortion laws are in your state. A Grown-Ass Woman knows her voice needs to be a part of both the local and national conversation; that her opinion about her to day-to-day life counts. Whether you're actively involved with your local selectmen or just a devoted voter, you're making your government work for you. And so when it's time to count the voices in the form of votes, yours is there, loud and proud.

grown-ass citizenship

★

BADGE of HONOR

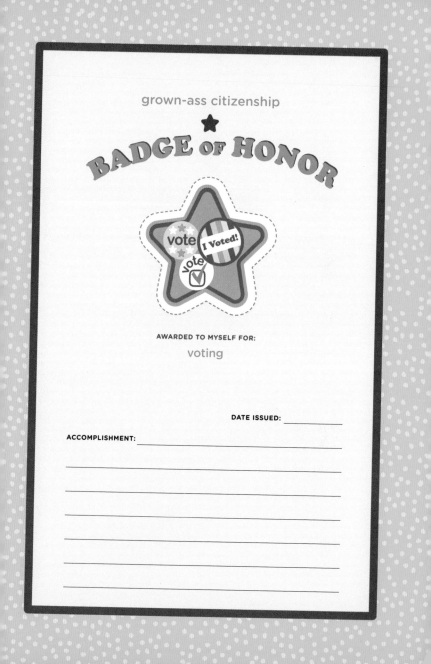

AWARDED TO MYSELF FOR:

voting

DATE ISSUED: _____

ACCOMPLISHMENT: _____

_____

_____

_____

_____

_____

_____

THE
safe-driver discount
BADGE

It's a two-ton hunk of metal and flammable liquids, and you have it under control, no big deal. When you do find yourself in a scrape, you handle it like an adult. But this badge isn't *just* for not crashing your vehicle into humans and through buildings and off of cliffs, it's for being able to handle the *whole driving package*.

You know about oil changes, tire changing, radiators that aren't in homes, off-road terrain, and seat warmer burn. Maybe you can identify a make and model from just the headlights, or maybe you can't, but you have done the work to become at least somewhat competent regarding your car. You are confident that if you need a new car, you will be able to purchase one without mortgaging a kidney or driving away in a deathtrap. And if all that fails, at least you got the right insurance. Drive safe!

grown-ass citizenship

★ BADGE OF HONOR

AWARDED TO MYSELF FOR:

handling driving and car maintenance

DATE ISSUED: _____

ACCOMPLISHMENT: _____

_____

_____

_____

_____

_____

_____

THE
✓ finishing what you start
BADGE

Sometimes it can be torturous to follow up on the tiny details of a project—to dot t's and cross i's when there are *brandnewshinyuntouched* ideas/jobs/people/projects to play with. But finishing what you start is something that Grown-Ass Women know how to do.

Reaching goals requires what experts call "follow-through," which, like "willpower," is an intangible force that might not exist at all. **But you have it!** The things you begin get to have endings. Your scarves are not half-unwoven, your gardens are not overgrown and dying, your friends are not waiting in a parking lot somewhere wondering why you didn't show up to brunch, and your novels even have epilogues. Take a step back and be proud of what you have **done.**

grown-ass citizenship

★

BADGE of HONOR

AWARDED TO MYSELF FOR:
finishing what i started

DATE ISSUED: _____

ACCOMPLISHMENT: _____

_____

_____

_____

_____

_____

_____

wait for this

A wise woman once said adulthood is a series of lines, and then you die. Okay, maybe no one said that, but sometimes it feels true.

Being a grown-up requires a completely annoying amount of patience. Whether you're trying to get through TSA pre-check, boarding the subway, or picking up a prescription at the pharmacy, most self-sufficient people find themselves in a queue at least once a week. Lines are how we keep a civilization civil, but they can feel dehumanizing, or at least infantilizing. You deserve a damn medal for all those lines, but you're more likely to get a crowded train car, or a surly clerk who has been dealing with a long line of frustrated people. At least you have this badge.

So kudos to you, Grown-Ass Woman. You earned this badge for standing in line, time after time, with patience and kindness, and for never ever cutting or yelling at the poor clerk about "bureaucracy."

dealing with life's tough moments

?!*!

BADGE OF HONOR

AWARDED TO MYSELF FOR:

patiently waiting in line

DATE ISSUED: _____

ACCOMPLISHMENT: _____

_____

_____

_____

_____

_____

_____

"how is a gal like you still single?"

What a good, insightful question! Were you wondering why a gal like me weighs a few extra pounds, or why a gal like me is in an entry-level job, or why a gal like me is making such quick work of this drink?

It's a shame that some people feel entitled to ask women discourteous and invasive questions. We're lobbying Congress to resolve this issue right now. But until that day, when someone else refuses to keep a conversation appropriate, you wrest it back to a place of normalcy. You manage to be gracious in the face of your boss/aunt/high school friend's bald-faced rudeness; expertly dodging, deflecting, changing the subject, and never giving some jerk information they don't deserve.

And when a line of inquiry is just too much, you deploy this great little trick: holding their gaze while saying, "What a strange question," and then brightly changing the subject to something more socially acceptable, like Netflix documentaries, how cute baby seals are, or how long everyone at the party can hold their breath.

dealing with life's tough moments

?!*!

BADGE OF HONOR

AWARDED TO MYSELF FOR:

being gracious in the face of rude questions

DATE ISSUED: _____

ACCOMPLISHMENT: _____

_____

_____

_____

_____

_____

_____

THE
levelheadedness
BADGE

Sure, you write that angry email, the one that says all the things you've needed to say and would definitely be fired/dumped/permanently banned from the movie theater for. But you don't send it! You are a person who takes a step back and breathes.

It can be hard to be levelheaded sometimes. The world is agitating: people are silly or willfully ignorant, institutions are broken, systems are bad, and even in the age of smartphones, telemarketers still exist. But despite all this, you keep your cool. You take a walk around the block instead of yelling at your pig-headed coworker; you refuse to fight for a parking space or cab, knowing there are more in the world; you don't save up the terrible burn that would destroy your boyfriend or your mom, you let it go and forget it; and when you fight, you try to see both sides. Not losing your cool means you have so much cool to give. Stay sane!

dealing with life's tough moments

?!*!

BADGE OF HONOR

AWARDED TO MYSELF FOR:

being levelheaded

DATE ISSUED: _____

ACCOMPLISHMENT: _____

_____

_____

_____

_____

_____

_____

THE
extreme weather
BADGE

It is a terrible fact that life doesn't stop in the winter. Or the summer. Or during intense rain or overwhelming wind. But you're still getting done all that you normally get done—on ice (or while sweating or dripping, and despite losing your best hat). The elements add additional chores to our lives: we have to add snow tires and knit scarves, fix AC units, slog through puddles, and push against the punishing gale, uphill both ways. We arrive at our jobs after harrowing commutes, pouring sweat, laden with icicles, windblown, and exhausted. But the world slowly turns on, moving incrementally toward a different season or a different day, and you still have a life to lead! Get out there and be your own force of nature. Warm up the winter with your laugh and cool down the summer with well-chilled beverages.

dealing with life's tough moments

?!*!

BADGE OF HONOR

AWARDED TO MYSELF FOR:

handling extreme weather

DATE ISSUED: _____

ACCOMPLISHMENT: _____

_____

_____

_____

_____

_____

_____

"just want to hide my face"book

for social media angst

These days, it's a rite of passage to humiliate ourselves on the internet. Whether it's a blackout pic posted by an old roommate or an ill-advised debate with a Twitter troll, we've all found ourselves upset about something because it's on the internet. But the truth is, the internet is where we live now and we're just as likely to embarrass ourselves on it as we are to fall down a flight of stairs upon entering a party full of strangers on a first date.

You *truly* earn this badge when you take a rough situation in stride. You realize that 1) by being hard on yourself, you're only compounding any hurt you feel, and 2) you are far from the only person to have a negative internet-related experience. Whether you need to stand up for yourself, or stand down, you take steps to move past this situation. And when all else fails, you're only a few clicks away from cute animal pictures.

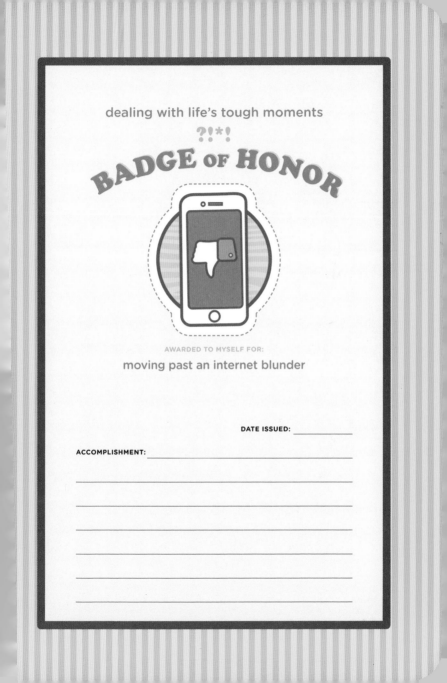

dealing with life's tough moments

?!*!

BADGE OF HONOR

AWARDED TO MYSELF FOR:

moving past an internet blunder

DATE ISSUED: _____

ACCOMPLISHMENT: _____

_____

_____

_____

_____

_____

_____

THE
we all go a little
mad sometimes
BADGE

Feeling like you don't have a great grip on the world happens to everyone sometimes. Whether you're feeling anger, anxiety, paranoia, sadness, fear, suspicion, or just plain strange and unprovable thoughts, living in the world provokes a range of reactions, and when yours isn't in line with everyone else's it can be confusing and scary. What's important is that you take care of yourself and your mental health, and don't beat yourself up for having a difficult time. Maybe it's reading your horoscope daily, maybe it's having an unshakeable fear of men in yellow hats, maybe it's feeling moods and thoughts you can't control. You're not alone, you're never beyond help, and you're still a cool gal.

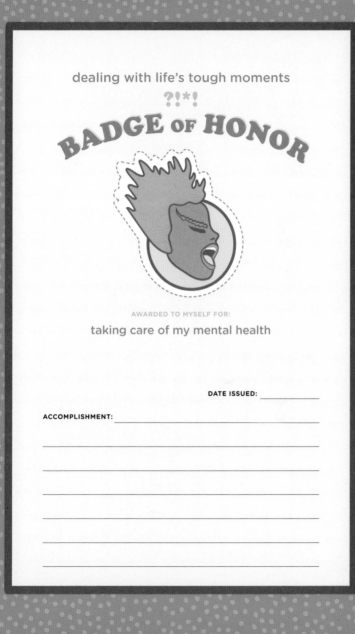

dealing with life's tough moments

?!*!

BADGE of HONOR

AWARDED TO MYSELF FOR:

taking care of my mental health

DATE ISSUED: _____

ACCOMPLISHMENT: _____

_____

_____

_____

_____

_____

_____

new year, new you

A lot about New Year's is kind of dumb—the expectations, the anticipation, the stress, the silly glasses (kidding, those are great). At the *end* of the day, it's usually another day where nothing really changes. Well, at the end of the day, everyone you know is really drunk.

BUT the solar calendar and popular social custom award us all a new chance to remake ourselves and our lives, and we should take our free chances where we can get them. Sure, it doesn't really matter if you decide to better yourself on January 1st or April 23rd or August 11th, but it's always nice to try to be the best you you can be! If you didn't start on the first, NBD! Your New Year is whenever you make it, as long as you're serious about setting big goals and achieving them. Putting yourself on a path to happiness and success is the newest year of all. It's not an easy road, but it's an impressive one. Happy New You!

holidays

BADGE of HONOR

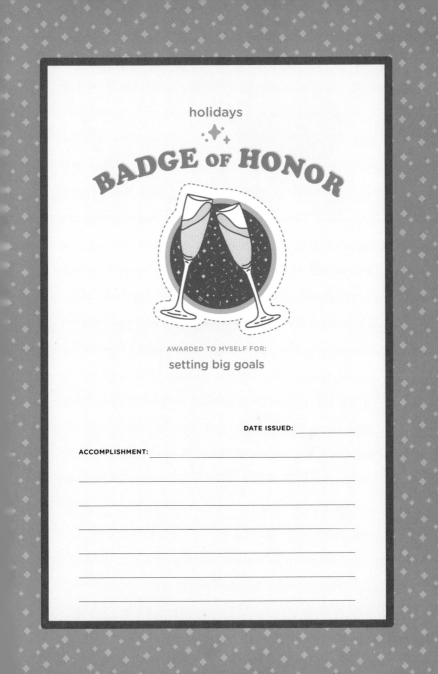

AWARDED TO MYSELF FOR:

setting big goals

DATE ISSUED: _____

ACCOMPLISHMENT: _____

_____

_____

_____

_____

_____

_____

being cool about valentine's day

Maybe you're alone on Valentine's Day. You know what's wrong with that? You're right, literally nothing.

Or maybe you're coupled up. You know what's amazing about that? Eh, some things, but not enough to act like a big jerk to single people! And definitely not enough to behave badly or put a lot of unnecessary stress on your significant person.

You're fantastic, and you deserve to have another person by your side if you want one. But you also know that 1) there's a *lot* more to you than that and 2) today is just one day! Out of so many days in your whole life!

No matter what happens, you'll spend time with someone great today. You!

holidays

BADGE OF HONOR

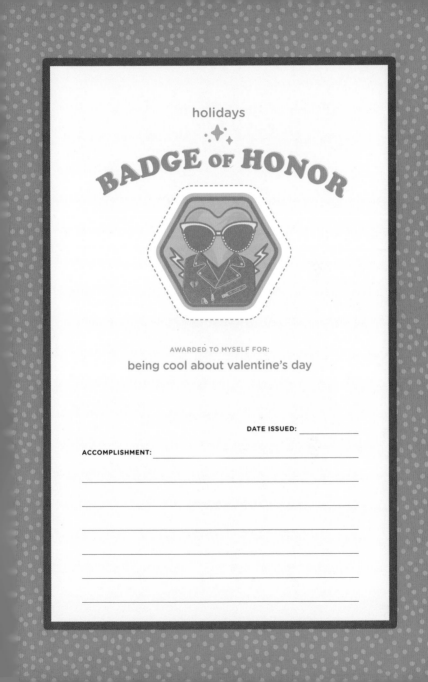

AWARDED TO MYSELF FOR:

being cool about valentine's day

DATE ISSUED: _____

ACCOMPLISHMENT: _____

_____

_____

_____

_____

_____

_____

unsexy costume

There's nothing wrong with a sexy costume because fun is fun, but there's something excellent about a chick who, on the boobsiest day of the year, shows up in a bear costume that covers her from head to toe. Seeing a woman go balls to the wall on a costume that does not exist primarily to make people want to remove it is refreshing. Plus: fewer nip-slips.

If you're stuck for ideas this Halloween, here are some unsexed-up costumes:

Miss Havisham	**MSNBC**
Jodie Foster in *Nell*	**Harriet the Spy**
Mother Teresa	**Our impending mortality**
A sea monster	**Your own Nana**

Even if you're dressed as the sexy version of your own Nana (oh girl, why), a sense of humor goes a long way, any day of the year. You get points for sex appeal—sex appeal from how damn funny you are.

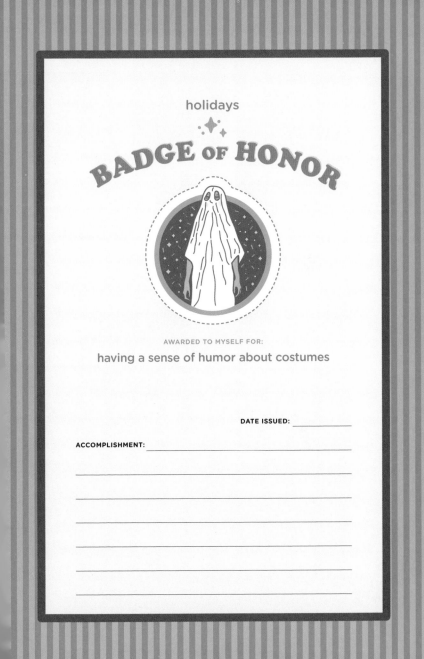

holidays

BADGE OF HONOR

AWARDED TO MYSELF FOR:

having a sense of humor about costumes

DATE ISSUED: _____

ACCOMPLISHMENT: _____

_____

_____

_____

_____

_____

_____

surviving thanksgiving

When the holidays are upon us, they can really feel up *on* us, smothering a Grown-Ass Woman with weight and pressure and expectation. Thanksgiving is a great time for turkey (cooked, and Wild), stuffing (seasoned, and what we do to our emotions), rolls (buttered, and the kind your aunt gets on when she's been drinking), and cranberry sauce (just cranberry sauce—that stuff is awesome). But the stress might also come from being far from home and carving (you get it) out your own traditions, or from attending the celebration of another family for the first time (Godspeed).

Thanksgiving really is about being thankful (oh, *that's* why they call it that), so take some time today to find what you appreciate, and celebrate that gratitude. Whether your holiday celebration is a welcome reprieve from the daily grind, or a nice reminder of why you're thankful to have other days in the year, just know that you'll make it through, and that cranberry sauce is delicious.

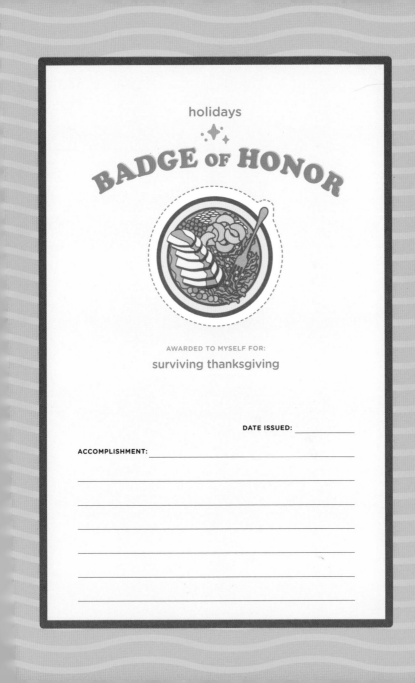

holidays

BADGE of HONOR

AWARDED TO MYSELF FOR:

surviving thanksgiving

DATE ISSUED: _____

ACCOMPLISHMENT: _____

_____

_____

_____

_____

_____

_____

_____

ISBN 978-1-4521-6150-1

Manufactured in China

Design by Sara Schneider

Chronicle Books publishes distinctive books and gifts.
From award-winning children's titles, bestselling cookbooks,
and eclectic pop culture to acclaimed works of art and design,
stationery, and journals, we craft publishing that's instantly
recognizable for its spirit and creativity. Enjoy our publishing
and become part of our community at
www.chroniclebooks.com.

10 9 8 7 6 5 4 3 2

CHRONICLE BOOKS
680 SECOND STREET
SAN FRANCISCO, CA 94107